The Algonquin

by Natalie M. Rosinsky

Content Adviser: Bruce Bernstein, Ph.D., Assistant Director for Cultural Resources,
National Museum of the American Indian, Smithsonian Institution

Reading Adviser: Rosemary G. Palmer, Ph.D.,
Department of Literacy, College of Education,
Boise State University

COMPASS POINT BOOKS
MINNEAPOLIS, MINNESOTA

Compass Point Books
3109 West 50th Street, #115
Minneapolis, MN 55410

Visit Compass Point Books on the Internet at *www.compasspointbooks.com*
or e-mail your request to *custserv@compasspointbooks.com*

On the cover: A 1913 Algonquin birch bark basket from the Mattawa Band

Photographs ©: Canadian Museum of Civilization, photographer Merle Toole, catalogue no. III-L-191 a-b,
image no. S97-2354, cover; Courtesy Algonquin Nation Secretariat, 4, 36, 37, 39, 40, 41, 43; Canstock Images
Inc./Index Stock Imagery, 5; Canadian Heritage Gallery ID20046/National Archives of Canada C24379, 9;
Canadian Heritage Gallery ID10057/National Archives of Canada C-40198, 10; North Wind Picture Archives,
11, 24, 27, 29, 30, 31, 33; Marilyn "Angel" Wynn, 12–13, 14, 20–21, 25, 34; National Archives of Canada,
C-040293, 15; Canadian Museum of Civilization, catalogue no. III-L-279 a-b, image no. S93-7862, 17;
Canadian Museum of Civilization, catalogue no. III-L-276, image no. S2003-3405, 18; Corel, 19; Marilyn
"Angel" Wynn/Library of Congress, 22; Mary Evans Picture Library, 23; Canadian Heritage Gallery
ID20049/C.W. Jefferys/National Archives of Canada C103059, 26; John C. Knox/National Archives of
Canada/PA-029343, 35; John Cross/The Free Press, 48.

Creative Director: Terri Foley
Managing Editor: Catherine Neitge
Photo Researcher: Svetlana Zhurkina
Designer/Page production: Bradfordesign, Inc./Les Tranby
Cartographer: XNR Productions, Inc.
Educational Consultant: Diane Smolinski

Library of Congress Cataloging-in-Publication Data
Rosinsky, Natalie M. (Natalie Myra)
    The Algonquin / by Natalie M. Rosinsky.
        p. cm. — (First reports)
Includes index.
    ISBN 0-7565-0642-5 (hardcover)
    1. Algonquin Indians—History—Juvenile literature. 2. Algonquin Indians—
    Social life and customs—Juvenile literature. I. Title. II. Series.
    E99.A349R67 2005
971.3004'9733—dc22   2004000589

Table of Contents

*NOTE: In this book, words that are defined in the glossary are in **bold** the first time they appear in the text.*

Who Are the Algonquin?

△ *Young girls sing and play traditional Algonquin hand drums during National Aboriginal Day, which celebrates Canada's native people.*

The Algonquin (al-GON-kin) are a native people of the northern woodlands who today live in the eastern part of Canada. More than 8,000 Algonquin live in the **provinces** of Quebec and Ontario.

Most Algonquin live in one of 10 communities. Each community is located on a **reserve.** There are

▲ *The Algonquin's home in eastern Canada's northern woodlands*

nine reserves in southern Quebec and one in western Ontario. Waterways are **traditionally** important to this people. Their many lakes, rivers, and streams are only a small part of land the Algonquin once inhabited.

The name *Algonquin* means "at the place of spearing fishes and eels" in another Indian language. In their own language, the Algonquin call themselves the *Anishnabe*. This means the "people."

The Algonquin call their own language *Anishnabemowin*. Yet the words *Algonquin* and *Algonquian* are also used to describe a large family of languages. The speakers of these languages once lived across a wide area. They were members of many different tribes.

The double meanings of Algonquin or Algonquian sometimes cause mix-ups. Yet the Algonquin people of eastern Canada are the tribe that uses the name Algonquin today.

The Algonquin came to Canada about 500 years ago. They had lived on the mid-Atlantic seaboard, but other tribes forced the Algonquin to move west.

The Algonquin tribe has grown to its present

▲ *A map of past and present Algonquin lands shows the 10 current reserves.*

number after many losses. It is believed that there were 6,000 Algonquin in 1600, but only about 1,500 Algonquin by the mid-1700s.

Hunters and Gatherers

In the past, the Algonquin were hunters and gatherers. Each family had its own hunting territory of 20 to 40 square miles (52 to 104 square kilometers). In fall, winter, and spring, families traveled within their territories. They followed the moose, deer, and black bear that they depended upon for their food.

Only the men hunted these animals. Beaver and waterbirds were also favorite foods. The skins and fur from these animals were used for clothing, houses, and household items.

In the summer, the Algonquin came together at a home camp they shared with other families in their **band.** The camp was usually by a lake or river. There, women and children picked ripe berries. They gathered other plants that were good to eat. The Algonquin traded with others, and stored food for the winter. The Algonquin who lived farthest south grew corn.

▲ *An Algonquin hunter calls a moose.*

△ *An Algonquin family travels by toboggan and snowshoes.*

In the winter, the Algonquin sometimes wore snowshoes for travel. They pulled toboggans filled with their belongings over ice or snow-covered ground.

Throughout the year, the water-rich land made fish an important food for the Algonquin. In the winter, they drilled holes in frozen lakes and streams and went ice fishing.

▲ *The Algonquin built birch bark canoes.*

The Algonquin also used waterways to travel. They built and used fast, light canoes. These boats had wood frames. Around the frames, the Algonquin wrapped thin sheets of bark stripped from birch trees.

Algonquin houses, or wigwams, were often made of birch bark as well. These lightweight houses had wooden support poles covered in bark. In winter, layers of warm animal hides might be added.

Wigwams were usually cone-shaped or round. They could be taken apart quickly when hunters needed to travel.

Wigwams were easy to put together when families stopped at night. At their summer camping places, the Algonquin sometimes built larger wigwams or lodges. These had room for visitors.

Thin sheets of birch bark were useful in other ways, too. They were used to make baskets, toys, and dolls.

Women even carried babies tied safely to cradle boards called *tikinagan* made partly of birch bark.

▲ *Wigwams with wooden frames were easy to put together and take apart.*

Family and Everyday Life

△ *An Algonquin woman holds a baby in a decorated cradleboard.*

▲ *An 1860 watercolor painting shows an Algonquin family camp.*

The immediate family of parents, children, and grandparents was important in Algonquin life. To the Algonquin, a father's family was most important.

Algonquin men held the right to hunt within a certain territory. When a father died, this right passed to his sons.

During cold weather, some families traveled and hunted alone. Sometimes, two or three related families traveled together.

In the summer, though, many families might band together to help one another hunt, gather, harvest, and enjoy each other's company. People might marry then, when the group was large.

Algonquin women made clothing from animal skins. They sewed with thread made from strings of tough animal flesh called sinews. They used sharpened animal bones for needles.

Women wore wraparound dresses. Men wore short clothes called breechcloths around the lower part of their bodies. In cold weather, they wore leggings as well.

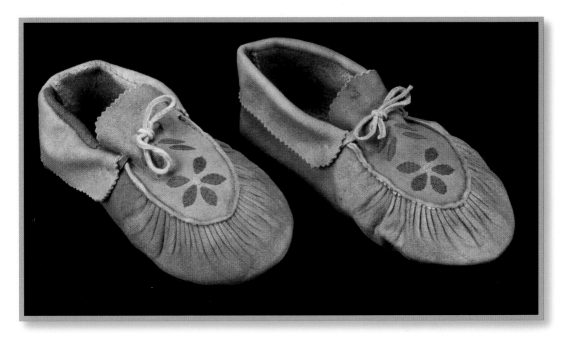

▲ *The Algonquin wore leather moccasins.*

In the winter, both men and women wore warm hide capes. The Algonquin protected their feet and kept them warm with leather moccasins.

The Algonquin often used wood and stone, as well as bones, for their tools. These included **awls,** axes, and hunting bows and arrows. They used animal teeth to shape thin strips of wood into fishing nets. The Algonquin made birch bark containers in many sizes and shapes. Sometimes, they would lightly carve designs on these containers.

Children played with dolls, tops, and other toys made of wood. Some girls had small cradle boards just for their dolls.

The Algonquin told many stories about their world. These stories were intended to teach lessons about being a good person, family member, and Algonquin.

One such Algonquin story said that bears once

An Algonquin doll cradle board
from the 18th century

had long tails. Supposedly, a fox tricked a greedy bear. The fox lied and said he caught fish by sticking his long tail into an ice-fishing hole. When the bear tried this, fish ate his tail! From then on, bears had short tails. Algonquin children learned through this story not to be greedy.

▲ *The Algonquin tell a story of how the bear lost his tail.*

Leaders in Peace and War

The leader of each band was always a man. This chief was called *ogima*. The ogima was chosen for his skills and courage. Because Algonquin families did not hunt as a band, the ogima did not make everyday decisions for families. The father did. If two or more families hunted together, the best hunter would lead them.

At summer gatherings, the ogima would make decisions about trade between groups. He would make decisions about war. Between 1570 and 1600, the Algonquin fought with the Mohawk and the Iroquois peoples. Sometimes, the Huron people were **allies** of the Algonquin. These wars were about territory and keeping trade agreements.

▲ *The best hunter would lead Algonquin families.*

Another kind of leader was also important within each Algonquin band. This person was the religious leader called a shaman. He was believed to have special knowledge and powers. For these, the shaman was both respected and feared. People asked for his help in times of peace and war.

△ *An Algonquin shaman mixes medicine for a cure.*

The Creation

The Algonquin believed that the world was created by one great being or god. They also believed that the world was inhabited by less-powerful spirits. The shaman, it was said, could help someone act in ways that pleased the spirits. He was also supposed to

▲ *The Algonquin believed a shaman could heal illnesses caused by evil spirits.*

help people understand their dreams. The shaman was supposed to be able to heal the sick. The Algonquin believed that evil spirits caused illness and accidents.

Stories were told about Wieshkay, who was part of the creation of the world. He sometimes took the form of a rabbit and liked to trick people! These stories helped the Algonquin understand how the world came to be. Wieshkay's mischief is a reminder of both the spirit world and what might happen if people misbehave.

△ *The Algonquin's stories helped them understand their world.*

▲ *The Algonquin smoked a pipe while praying and telling stories.*

When the Algonquin prayed, they would smoke a pipe. This pipe might be made of stone or wood. It was filled with tobacco. This was considered a sacred plant. The Algonquin believed smoking tobacco was a way to send their prayers. It was a way to give thanks to their great god. The Algonquin told stories about the spirits. During these times, they would also smoke a pipe.

△ *Explorer Samuel de Champlain traded with the native people.*

French fur traders first met the Algonquin in the 16th century. These traders were eager to have beaver fur from Algonquin territory. In Europe, this fur was used in fancy clothing. In 1608, the French explorer Samuel de Champlain signed a **treaty** with an Algonquin chief named Tessouat. It said that Champlain and his soldiers would help the Algonquin fight their enemies. In return, the Algonquin would be allies of the French.

As a result of the treaty, more French people arrived to live in the area that Champlain

▲ *A French priest preaches to the native people.*

called Quebec. This area included the territory of the Algonquin. Priests or **missionaries** who wanted to convert the Indians to Christianity also traveled to Quebec. Many native people did convert, but many did not. The Algonquin and other tribes caught terrible diseases from Europeans. Many native people died from the disease called smallpox.

As Indians died, more Europeans moved into the Algonquin's territory. Iroquois hunters increasingly used Algonquin land, too.

The Algonquin remained allies of the French. They helped them fight the British, who wanted to control more land and trade in North America. The Algonquin joined other Indian allies of the French in a war against Britain. It was called the French and Indian War. It lasted from 1756 to 1763.

In 1760, the British won a big battle. They gained control of Algonquin territory. The Algonquin then signed a new treaty. They agreed to be allies of the British. The British continued to win battles. In 1763, the French stopped fighting. The British had won the war. They now controlled Canada.

▲ *The Algonquin sided with the French in the French and Indian War.*

British Soldiers, Settlers, and Loggers

In 1763, the British king promised the Algonquin that they could keep their land. This promise would be broken many times.

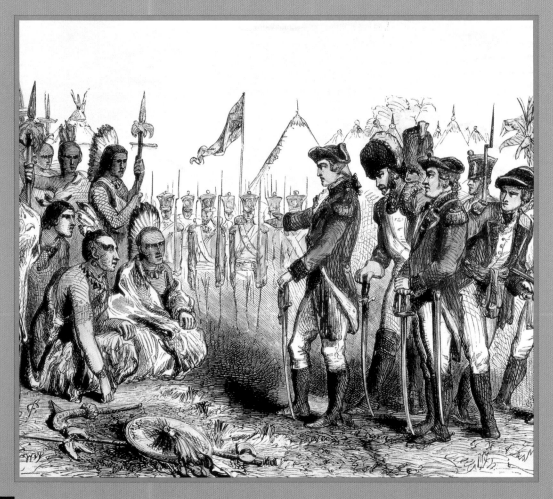

△ *The Algonquin sided with the British during the American Revolution.*

▲ *The British gave Algonquin chiefs a medal*
after the American Revolution.

The Algonquin remained allies of the British, however. When American colonists wanted independence from Britain, the Algonquin declared war on the colonists. The American **Revolution** lasted from 1775 to 1783. During this war, the Algonquin fought alongside the British and lost many men. The United States of America became a separate country. The Algonquin's traditional enemy, the Iroquois, had sided with the winning American colonists. This spelled further trouble for the Algonquin.

The colonists who supported the British government did not want independence. After the Revolution, these people moved to Canada. Many of them settled on Algonquin land. This broke the royal promise, but the British government did not stop these settlers.

The Algonquin still remained British allies. They fought alongside British soldiers in the War of 1812. The United States won this war in 1814.

Even though the Algonquin had been **loyal,** the British government again broke its word. In 1822, the British government bought some of the Algonquin's traditional land from the Mississaugas, another Indian tribe that did not own it. The British government paid the other tribe for the Algonquin land.

In the 1840s, lumber companies moved onto parts of Algonquin territory. They began to chop down the trees. The government did not stop these companies.

In 1851, Canadian officials passed laws setting up the first Algonquin reserves. These original reserves, though, were smaller than the land the Algonquin had been using. These reserves were meant to protect Algonquin land from further harm and loss. Again, promises were not kept. The Algonquin continued to lose territory. New laws and decisions made by judges took still more land away from the Algonquin.

▲ Logs were stored near Quebec in the 1850s. The timber industry cut down trees on Algonquin land.

A New Country and Problems

△ *Algonquin in front of their wigwam in the 19th century*

Canada became a nation separate from Great Britain in 1867. It became fully independent of Great Britain in the 1930s. Yet neither of these changes helped the Algonquin people much.

In the 1880s and 1890s, people hunting for sport killed many moose, deer, bear, and beaver. These important Algonquin foods became scarce.

Lumber companies continued to destroy woodlands. In the 20th century, the Algonquin lost more hunting territory as new dams flooded some of the land. The Canadian government supported these dams. They were part of power plants that provided electricity. New highways also cut into traditional Algonquin territory. Sometimes, Algonquin hunters had problems because the provinces of Quebec and Ontario had different laws about hunting.

▲ *The Algonquin lost land when dams flooded their territory.*

The Canadian government set up a Department of Indian Affairs. It was supposed to protect all of the country's native peoples. Yet the department's workers did not always do their job. Some government Indian **agents** helped the Algonquin. Many did not.

△ Ottawa's Parliament buildings stand behind an interpretive center tepee on Victoria Island. Canada's capital may have gotten its name from an Algonquin word for trade, atawa.

The Algonquin Today

Today, the Algonquin are speaking out about their concerns. Three communities have formed the Algonquin Nation Tribal **Council.** This organization represents the people of Timiskaming, Wolf Lake, and Barriere Lake. Other communities are represented by the Algonquin Anishinabeg Nation. These

▲ *Grand Chief Carol McBride (in white) and other chiefs have spoken out about tribal concerns.*

two groups give Algonquin people a voice in the **Assembly** of First Nations. This organization represents all of Canada's native peoples. It speaks for them at world meetings held by the United Nations. It also works with the Canadian government.

In 1991, Canada accepted an agreement supported by the United Nations and the Assembly of First Nations. Canada agreed that its native peoples should have more power over their own traditional lands. This **Trilateral** Agreement between the Algonquin of Barriere Lake, the provincial government of Quebec, and the federal government of Canada is still being developed and has not yet been signed.

Since 2000, the Algonquin have protested a large garbage dump that is to be built near them in Ontario. In 2001, Grand Chief Carol McBride and others protested the logging plans of lumber companies that affect the Algonquin's traditional way of life.

▲ *Algonquin from Barriere Lake look over a map of the Trilateral Agreement area.*

△ *The Algonquin manage their own schools on the reserves.*

Today, the Algonquin people are citizens of Canada. On their reserves, many government services, such as schools and health care, are managed by the Algonquin themselves.

Each Algonquin band has its own elected chief. The Algonquin Nation Tribal Council is overseen by a grand chief and one chief from each community.

Many Algonquin still earn money trapping animals. Unemployment, though, remains a problem

▲ *An Algonquin builds a birch bark canoe in the traditional manner of his ancestors.*

in many Algonquin communities. Some communities still need better roads and other basic government services. As they work to solve these modern problems, the Algonquin people keep hold of their traditions.

They draw upon their own ancient teachings. They collect the stories of their elders.

They also teach their own language in their schools. More than 60 percent of the Algonquin speak Anishnabemowin, along with French or English, which are both spoken in Canada.

The Algonquin have hope for the future because they are growing in numbers. Through their own efforts, they are overcoming centuries of terrible treatment and broken promises. The Algonquin are reestablishing self-rule through their own language and their own government.

▲ An Algonquin girl from Timiskaming holds her little pet rat. In school, Algonquin children learn their own language as well as English or French.

Glossary

agents—people who work for someone or something else

allies—people or countries who agree to help each other in times of trouble

assembly—a group of people meeting for a specific purpose

awls—small pointed tools for making holes in things

band—a group of people who live together or are part of a tribe

council—a group of people chosen to make important decisions

loyal—remaining faithful to someone, an idea, or a country

missionaries—people who travel to teach their religion

provinces—divisions of some countries; Canada has 10 provinces and three territories

reserve—a large area of land set aside for native people; in the United States, reserves are called reservations

revolution—a war by people against those who have controlled them

traditionally—how a group of people has done things for a long time

treaty—an agreement between two governments

trilateral—involving three groups or things

Did You Know?

- The words *canoe* and *toboggan* come from the Algonquin language.

- Today's Olympic sport called luge is a form of tobogganing.

- Algonquin baskets were once decorated with the royal sign of France, the lily, called the *fleur de lis.*

- Two Algonquin men, John Chabot and Gino Odjick, played in the National Hockey League.

At a Glance

Tribal name: Anishnabe

Divisions: In Quebec: Pikogan (Abitibiwinni), Lac Simon, Timiskaming, Winneway (Long Point), Barriere Lake, Grand Lac Victoria (Kitcisakik), Wolf Lake, Kipawa (Eagle Village), and Kitigan Zibi; In Ontario: Golden Lake (Pikwakanagan).

Past locations: Ottawa River valley on the border between Quebec and Ontario

Present locations: Quebec and Ontario, Canada

Traditional houses: birch bark wigwams

Traditional clothing materials: animal skins

Traditional transportation: birch bark canoes, foot, toboggans, snowshoes

Traditional food: fish, moose, bear, beaver, ducks and geese, berries

Important Dates

1500	Algonquin move west from land along the Atlantic coast.
1500s	French fur traders meet the Algonquin.
1570–1600	Algonquin at war with the Mohawk and the Iroquois tribes.
1608	Samuel de Champlain signs treaty with the Algonquin.
1756–1763	French and Indian War against the British; Algonquin are French allies until British gain control of Quebec.
1760	Algonquin sign treaty with the British.
1775–1783	Algonquin are British allies during the American Revolution.
1783	American colonists who sided with British move onto Algonquin land.
1812–1814	Algonquin are British allies during the War of 1812.
1822	Canadian officials purchase Algonquin lands from the Mississaugas, another tribe.
1851	Canadian government establishes first Algonquin reserves.
1991	Trilateral agreement accepted; its outcome will have a major impact on all native peoples.

Want to Know More?

At the Library

Martin, Rafe. *The Rough-Face Girl.* New York: G. P. Putnam's Sons, 1992.

McCurdy, Michael. *An Algonquian Year: The Year According to the Full Moon.* Boston: Houghton Mifflin Co., 2000.

Shemie, Bonnie. *Houses of Bark: Tipi, Wigwam, and Longhouse.* Montreal, Canada: Tundra Books, 1990.

On the Web

For more information on the Algonquin, use FactHound to track down Web sites related to this book.

1. Go to *www.facthound.com*
2. Type in a search word related to this book or this book ID: 0756506425.
3. Click on the *Fetch It* button.

Your trusty FactHound will fetch the best Web sites for you!

On the Road

Obadjiwan–Fort Témiscamingue
834 Vieux Fort Road
Ville Marie, Quebec
Canada J9V 1N7
800/463-6769
To visit a national historic site that was a summer gathering place of the Algonquin and their ancestors for more than 1,000 years and later a major trading post

Index

About the Author

Natalie M. Rosinsky writes about history, social studies, economics, science, and other fun things. One of her two cats usually sits on her computer as she works in Mankato, Minnesota. Natalie earned graduate degrees from the University of Wisconsin and has been a high school and college teacher.